SO-BZE-876

A Closer Look at
EARLY CHINA

A CLOSER LOOK BOOK
© The Archon Press Ltd
1977

Originated and designed by
David Cook and Associates
and produced by
The Archon Press Ltd
28 Percy Street
London W1P 9FF

First published in
Great Britain 1977 by
Hamish Hamilton
Children's Books Ltd
90 Great Russell Street
London WC1B 3PT

The author wishes to
acknowledge the assistance
received from Arthur
Cotterell, Head of the
Department of Adult
Education, North Herts
College, during the
preparation of this book.

0 241 89561 8

Printed in Great Britain by
W. S. Cowell Ltd
Butter Market, Ipswich

A closer LOOK at EARLY CHINA

Wendy Boase

Illustrated by

Angus McBride and Terry Dalley

Hamish Hamilton · London

The Middle Kingdom

Yin and Yang

The Chinese believed that true harmony in the universe depended on a balance between the forces of *Yin* and *Yang*. *Yin* represented everything negative, female, dark and of the Earth. *Yang* was positive, male, light, Heaven. The two forces were visualised as a circle divided into two equal parts by a curved line.

The design expresses the idea of *Yin* and *Yang* existing in a delicate balance, not in conflict with one another. Evils such as droughts or floods or war were thought to be caused by a temporary imbalance between the two. All men tried to live according to the theory of *Yin* and *Yang*.

Yu the Great leaves home
According to legend, Yu the Great Engineer was the first man to control China's rivers. He deepened the channels to contain floods and to irrigate the land. It is said that he laboured for 13 years without once going into his house to rest.

Traditionally, the Chinese have regarded their country as the centre of the world and the focus of civilisation. They called it the 'Middle Kingdom' and, although there were times when it was overrun by barbarians, it has remained an isolated and mysterious land throughout history. Under the Han Dynasty it stretched some 2000 kilometres from the Tibetan plateau to the east coast, and about the same distance from the Great Wall in the north to the southern borders. China is divided into regions by three great river systems: the West River in the south, the Yangtze River in the middle, and the Yellow River in the north. Over these three vast areas the climate ranges from sub-tropical to sub-arctic and land forms include high mountains, deep valleys and the huge river basins themselves. Yet this diverse country produced a self-contained civilisation which flourished for over 3000 years.

The first Chinese people settled along the turbulent Yellow River in the 'Land Within the Passes', a wedge of country covered with thick deposits of rich, yellow earth, called loess. The soil may have been good but early agricultural settlers suffered from unpredictable natural elements. They faced sparse rainfall, frost and snow as well as long droughts. Worst of all were the uncontrollable floods. To survive, the Chinese had to come to terms with Nature. Their desire to live and work in harmony with Nature was expressed in the ancient theory of *Yin* and *Yang*. The development of water control shows how this theory was applied in practice. Under the system of corvée (unpaid labour), peasants worked one month of every year in the state labour corps. They co-operated with Nature by digging deeper channels for the water to flow through to irrigate the fertile land which grew food for the 50 million inhabitants of the Middle Kingdom.

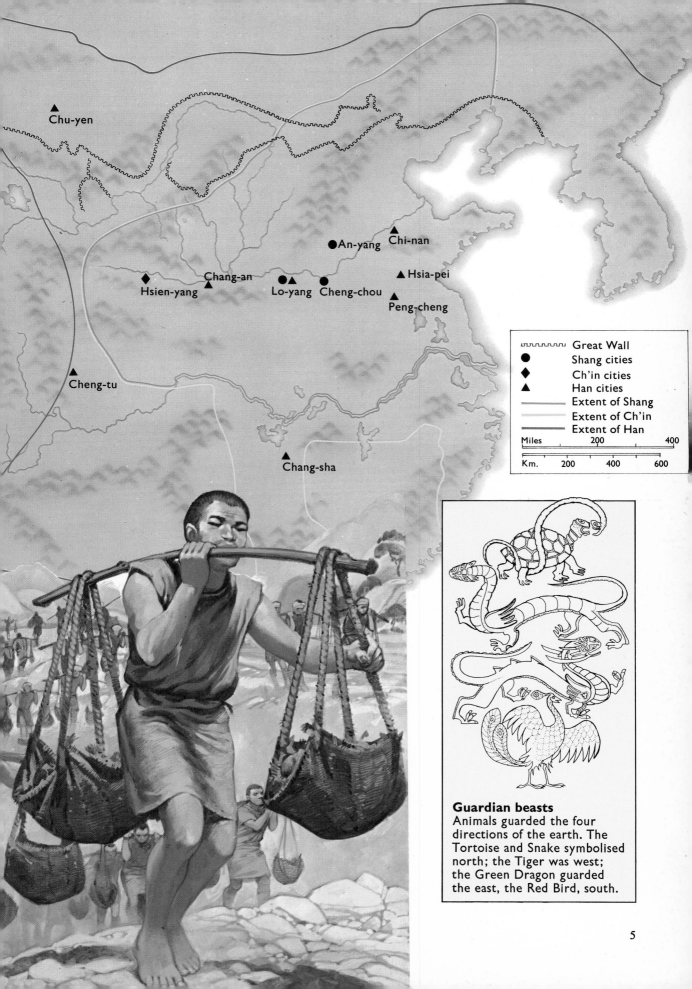

Chu-yen ▲

●An-yang   ▲Chi-nan

◆   ▲ Chang-an
Hsien-yang   ●● ▲   ● Cheng-chou   ▲ Hsia-pei
                    Lo-yang   ▲ Peng-cheng

▲
Cheng-tu

▲
Chang-sha

〰〰〰〰 Great Wall
● Shang cities
◆ Ch'in cities
▲ Han cities
—— Extent of Shang
—— Extent of Ch'in
—— Extent of Han

Miles   200   400
Km.   200   400   600

Guardian beasts
Animals guarded the four
directions of the earth. The
Tortoise and Snake symbolised
north; the Tiger was west;
the Green Dragon guarded
the east, the Red Bird, south.

5

The creation of the universe

In Chinese legend, the universe began as an egg. One day the egg cracked open and a man called P'an-ku was born. For centuries he grew taller and taller, one half of the broken egg-shell rising above him to form the sky, the other half remaining below him as the earth. After 18,000 years P'an-ku died, and the fragments of his body became the elements of Nature. His head formed the sun and moon, his breath the wind, his sweat the rain and his voice the thunder. Rivers and seas were made from his blood and mountains from his limbs. Lastly, the fleas on P'an-ku's body became the ancestors of mankind. This myth reflects the traditional Chinese view of man's modest position in the natural world, an idea which is often expressed in paintings.

The cosmic plan

Bronze mirrors of the late Chou and Han periods were covered with beautiful designs symbolising the Chinese idea of world order. The earth is represented by a square around a central knob. The T-shapes on each side of it are the sacred mountains which were thought to hold up the heavens. The surrounding circles, inscribed with mythical animals, flowers and scrolls, symbolise the outer edges of the universe. Harmony in the cosmos depended on the perfect balance between *Yin* and *Yang* – the negative and positive forces believed to act on all things. The *Yin-Yang* theory had an enormous influence on Chinese life and philosophy.

6

The origins of China

Half a million years ago, one of the ancestors of modern man, Pekin Man, lived in China. He could chip tools out of stone, make fire and speak simple words. In 1500 BC his descendants emerged into history under the Shang, the earliest Chinese dynasty, or family of kings, of which archaeological traces remain. According to Chinese myth, part of this vast time gap was filled by a number of legendary monarchs. First came P'an-ku, the creator, then the first king, Fu Hsi. He was followed by Shen Nung, patron of agriculture and medicine. Next came Huang Ti, the 'Yellow Emperor', under whose wise rule the arts and sciences flourished. The mythical age ends with Yu the Great Engineer, who became the first ruler of the Hsia dynasty.

No archaeological traces of the Hsia remain. But in the Yellow River valley – the 'Land Within the Passes' – the Shang left behind bronze vessels and written documents. So many artefacts were left there by their early successors that the area is called the cradle of Chinese civilisation. The Shang were conquered by the Chou, but it was not until 221 BC, under the Ch'in dynasty, that China became an empire, with a single authority ruling over the entire country. During the two thousand years of imperial history that followed the Ch'in, twenty-five dynasties have controlled China's destiny. The Han, founded by Liu Pang, is regarded as one of the most successful. Political unity, a rich cultural life, and the triumph of the philosophy of Confucianism characterised this period. Later dynasties were to look back with admiration on this golden Imperial Age.

The 'Yellow Emperor'
Huang Ti is regarded as the true founder of Chinese culture and the ancestor of all emperors.

The 'Divine Cultivator'
The first farmer, Shen Nung, is said to have ruled for 140 years.

Time Chart
The outer circle represents the flow of Chinese history, the inner periods of unrest or foreign occupation.

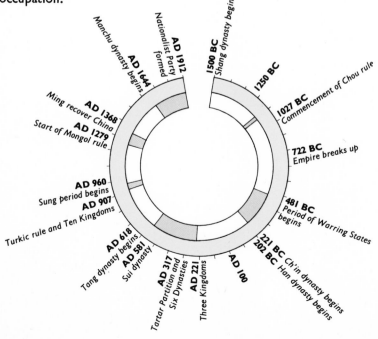

The first Han ruler
In 202 BC Liu Pang, a man of humble origins, controlled all the 'Land Within the Passes'. He became Emperor Han Kaotsu.

A turbulent sub-continent

The first history of China was written by Ssu-ma Ch'ien, the Imperial Astrologer at the court of Han Wu-ti (141–87 BC). According to this historian, the rise and fall of the Early Chinese dynasties followed an unending pattern. Each one began in good faith, then declined after several generations of rulers. Finally, the last cruel or weak king was overthrown by a new hero, and the cycle began again.

The first three Chinese dynasties recorded by Ssu-ma Ch'ien were the Hsia, the Shang and the Chou. The Hsia, traditionally founded by Yu the Great, may actually have flourished around 2000 BC, although there is no historical evidence of their existence. This legendary dynasty was followed by the Shang, who dominated the Middle Kingdom for about five centuries. On the flat plains of the Yellow River basin the Shang created a Bronze Age culture unmatched by any succeeding dynasty. They also wove silk, carved jade and ivory, and developed a written language. Their religion, based on ancestor worship, was to last for thousands of years.

However, the successful Shang eventually became corrupt and superstitious. In 1027 BC, the Chou, a family of warlike kings, swept out of the west to challenge them. Chou society saw a feudal golden age established, but once again repeated the pattern of success, decline and eventual collapse. After three centuries under their rule, China was plunged into more than 250 years of civil unrest. This so-called Warring States period ended in the military triumph of the Ch'in, who welded the country into a vast empire for the first time.

Although the First Empire lasted only a short time it had a profound effect on Chinese civilisation. A central government gradually weakened the old feudal society (one based on land ownership). Laws and the written language were standardised, as were weights and measures, farm tools and even the length of cart axles. Flood control, road- and bridge-building programmes were begun. The Great Wall was built to keep out the Hsiung-nu – the barbarian ancestors of the Huns. But the First Emperor, Shih Huang-ti, enforced his authority with such harsh laws and brutal punishments that rebellion broke out again. Liu Pang and the armies of the Han emerged victorious.

The quality of life under the Han Empire was superior to that of any previous dynasty. Paper had been invented; astronomers were charting the stars and recording sun-spots; water clocks, water pumps, seed-sowing machines and silk looms were in use. The Chinese began to trade their silk, gold and cast-iron for foreign pearls, glass, camels and donkeys. They absorbed new ideas from their neighbours, without revealing too many of the secrets of their own superb technology.

China was now the greatest power in Asia. The Hsiung-nu still posed a constant threat, but protected by an efficient cavalry and the crossbow – a weapon Europe was not to master for another thousand years – China enjoyed long periods of peace. The only break in four centuries of successful Han rule came when Wang Mang, an unpopular usurper, seized the throne in AD 9. His brief reign divides the great Empire into two periods: the Former Han (202 BC–AD 9) and the Later Han (AD 25–220).

The Heavenly Horses
China needed better horses so that her cavalry could outrun the hardy ponies of the Hsiung-nu. In Ferghana (Turkestan) a Han ambassador saw the 'Heavenly Horses', a spirited breed of animal like the one shown above. Emperor Han Wu-ti, having failed to negotiate with the barbarian king, sent 60,000 men to seize the animals by force. The king eventually agreed to exchange 3000 horses for a royal Chinese bride. Each horse was worth 300 pounds in gold.

China in turmoil
In 771 BC, the Chou rulers, harried by an alliance of barbarian tribes and rebel subjects, abandoned their capital after heavy fighting and fled further east to Loyang, where their dynasty, known as the Eastern Chou, survived for another 500 years, though in name only. During that time the different Chou states amalgamated until a small number of strong units emerged.

Weapons of war
The Shang army used curved bows, arrows, bronze daggers, axes and halberds – weapons with a double-edged, pointed blade fixed to a shaft at right angles. Han soldiers carried iron spears and swords, but their most deadly weapon was the crossbow.

9

The Han court
During the Han Dynasty the high position of the emperor in relation to the rest of his subjects was emphasised by the way in which he was housed. He lived behind the high walls of the Imperial Palace, secluded from common eyes, attended by servants, officials and special advisers. The emperor's life was usually strictly bound by elaborate formal ceremony. The clothes he wore, the food he ate, the design of the audience hall he sat in, were all regulated according to the seasons of the year or the forces dominant in Nature. Yet life at the Han court was not always governed by ritual, as this scene shows. While the emperor relaxes, government officials, soldiers and ladies of the court watch a cock-fight. A foreign ambassador, who has travelled perhaps from Asia or Korea with gifts for the emperor, passes the time in conversation with a courtier. In the foreground, a group of Confucian scholars talk quietly among themselves.

The heart of the empire

The people of Early China believed that their monarchs received the Mandate (authority to rule) directly from Heaven. They called the emperor 'Son of Heaven' and regarded him as the supreme authority on earth. He could expect obedience and loyalty from his subjects, but he was also responsible for their comfort and prosperity, and if he failed in his duties Heaven could withdraw its Mandate and bestow it on a new hero. This meant that although the right to the throne usually passed from father to son, an emperor's power depended on his own merits too.

The title of Emperor was created in 221 BC by Prince Cheng, the founder of the Ch'in Dynasty, who called himself Shih Huang-ti, the 'First Emperor'. The Ch'in Dynasty did not outlive its founder, but the ancient Chinese system of government did. It lasted for more than two thousand years and during that time the title of 'Emperor' was used by every Chinese ruler.

Although absolute power rested with the emperor and the central government, Han China was divided into smaller administrative kingdoms and provinces. The kings were appointed by the emperor, as were provincial governors and state officials who held their positions through their abilities. The highest ministers of state staffed imperial offices in the capital city. Lesser officials were responsible for palace security, the collection of taxes and tribute, the direction of public building, maintaining religious ceremonies and keeping historical records. These civil servants wore emblems on their caps and carried seals of gold, silver or bronze which indicated their ranks. The lesser officials, nobles, knights and scholars formed an elite class of Han society called the *shih*.

The next most important class was the *nung*, or peasants, because they produced the food on which the state depended. They were followed by the *kung*, the metal-workers and artists, whose work was considered less essential. The status of the *shang*, or merchants, who lived on trade, and soldiers, who manned the frontier, was much lower. Han society also included a few slaves.

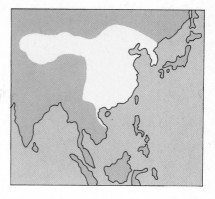

Imperial power
At the height of the Han empire Chinese influence reached right across Central Asia.

The framework of society
The chart illustrates the divisions of Han society in which people were valued according to the positive contributions they made.

The summer palace
A great city like Ch'ang-an often had several palaces, built throughout the centuries at the whim of the ruling emperor. Each palace probably had one or two audience halls and a number of separate towers and gates. A summer palace boasted artificial fountains or air conditioning, produced by mechanical fans blowing over ice-storage pits connected to ventilators in the rooms. Walking in the palace gardens was made pleasant by shady trees and streams of water flowing across smooth stones.

11

The backbone of the nation

The shaman
In primitive belief Nature was thought to be controlled by spirits. Contact with them could only be made by a shaman, a kind of medicine-man. His chief task was to bring rain to the fields.

Village homesteads
Walls are important in China and in ancient times all villages and every group of peasant huts within them were surrounded by mud walls. Earth walls of houses were sometimes plastered.

According to tradition, the first Chinese people lived like animals: they had no shelter or clothing and killed other animals for their food. But a wise man named Yu Tsao showed them how to build huts of branches and the legendary emperor, Shen Nung, is said to have taught them the art of farming. Since then, agriculture has been the basis of Chinese life and the *nung*, as the peasant-farmers were called, have been recognised as the backbone of society.

Despite his social importance, the life of the peasant was hard. He lived in a one-room house with an earth floor and no furniture. He tilled the yellow soil from dawn to dusk to provide food for both country and city, for soldiers fighting nomads on distant borders, and for the landowner who leased him the fields. A large part of his crop – grain in the north and rice in the south – went to the government in taxes. Floods and drought alternately threatened his very existence. His only hope of a better life lay in improved tools and more efficient irrigation. During the Han period a number of improvements were made – fields were split up into furrows and ridges and a new plough was introduced.

The introduction of iron and machinery made cultivation easier, but China's greatest achievement in agriculture was the control of water. When the sowing and harvesting were finished, the *nung* were mobilised under the ancient system of corvée, or unpaid labour, to build dams, waterways, irrigation canals and other public works. In 246 BC they completed the Chengkuo Canal which irrigated 400,000 acres of land, and they built the Kunghsien Canal which, 2000 years later, is still in operation. Two of the most massive achievements of the *nung* were the Great Wall and about 20,000 miles of road. Because the *nung* represented manpower on such a colossal scale, there was no need for an extensive system of slavery such as the Greeks and Romans used.

Ploughing
By the 5th century BC ox-drawn iron ploughshares were replacing clumsy wooden hand-ploughs.

Reaping
Scythes with cast-iron blades cut grain more efficiently than the older, stone reaping-knives.

Threshing
Machines increased output. Here a pedal-operated hammer is used to beat the husks off grain.

Labour-saving invention
The Chinese were using the wheelbarrow eleven centuries before it appeared in Europe.

Building an enclosure
Dry earth, held in a removable wooden frame, was rammed down until it formed a solid wall.

Cutting planks for building
Chinese workmen had a variety of saws, but the two-man frame saw was most effective.

Terraced slopes
Terraces prevent the rich loess soil of the Yellow River basin from being washed down from the hillsides. Loess only needs water to make it extremely fertile.

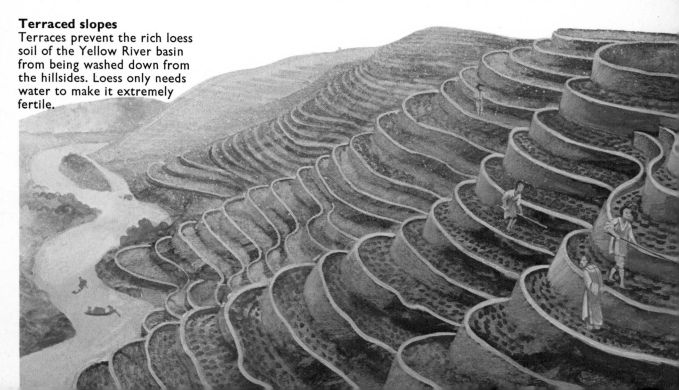

Ch'ang-an the capital city

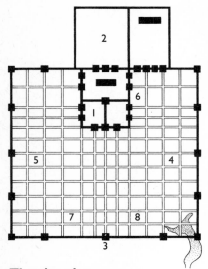

The city plan
From the Imperial Palace (1) and Park (2), the Imperial Way ran south to the Meng-ti Gate (3) and there were markets to the east (4) and west (5) of it. The privileged (6) lived near the Palace. Most citizens crowded into the small wards (7) and (8).

For centuries, Chinese storytellers have praised the wonders of Han Ch'ang-an: its jewelled palace, the Imperial Park full of rare animals, the ornamental towers and pleasure lakes, the ancestral shrines and religious temples. Chang Heng, an astronomer and poet of the 1st century, admired the capital and the care with which the Emperor Kao-tsu chose its site:

> For his purpose, he took thought of the spirits
>   of Heaven and Earth,
> That he might suitably determine the place that was
>   to be the Heavenly City.

The Chinese took great care in the planning of their cities. They were designed according to traditional beliefs about the order of the universe and the vital energies of Nature. Cities faced south, in the direction of *Yang*, symbol of strength and of the positive forces at work in the world. Their basic shape was a square, just as the earth itself was square in Chinese art. The palace, the home of the 'Son of Heaven', stood to the north of the city. The well-planned streets were divided up into 160 walled *li*, or wards. The nobles and officials lived nearest to the emperor. Most of the rest of the population was housed in the east, except for the *kung* (artisans), who lived and worked in the north and west, and the *shang* (merchants), who at first had to live outside the city walls. Thus the town plan was a symbol of the physical universe and of each man's place in it.

The emperor's palace and the religious buildings contrasted sharply with the humble homes of most of Ch'ang-an's citizens. Palaces were made of mud-brick, but their inner halls were lined with tiles and they were luxuriously furnished. Stone was rarely used for building, although the *Ming-t'ang*, or Hall of Brilliance, may have had a stone pavement or staircase. This hall was used for rituals involving the royal family. Houses were built of wood or mud-brick. They had courtyards and often gardens, too, where trees were planted among stones and water – both important to the Chinese as basic elements of the earth. Each house was surrounded by a wall and every ward was enclosed by another wall. Finally, the city itself was walled; twelve gates, each wide enough to take four carriages at once, led into the Heavenly City of Ch'ang-an.

15

The city streets

In the Imperial Age of China there were two great cities: Loyang and Ch'ang-an. The first, situated in the north-east on the River Lo, was the capital of the Former Han Dynasty (202 BC–AD 9). The latter, set in the strategic heart of the Land Within the Passes, was the capital of the Later Han Empire (AD 25–220). There were also many large provincial towns which served as administrative centres or army headquarters. In the Han period between 6 and 10 million people lived in these towns – as many as 250,000 of them in Ch'ang-an itself.

The capital city was the seat of government, the focus for all communications, and the commercial centre of China. It buzzed with activity: courtiers, officials, scholars, soldiers, workmen, peasants, beggars and thieves jostled each other in the streets. In the market places, passers-by were entertained by cock-fights and placed bets on their favourite birds. Copper and gold coins had begun to replace cowrie shells and bolts of silk as currency since the Warring States period. For their amusement, the rich preferred a day's hunting outside the city walls, trapping foxes, deer or pheasants and shooting at flocks of geese with bows and arrows.

The best in education could be found in the capital. An Imperial University was established in 124 BC and the sons of provincial officials came here to be trained for the civil service. At the time of the Emperor Han Huan-ti (147–68 BC), there were more than 30,000 students in Loyang.

The great city of Ch'ang-an fell with the collapse of the Han Empire. But the name Ch'ang-an means 'Long Security'. Four centuries later, in the T'ang dynasty it was restored to its former glory.

The city streets
The market places of Ch'ang-an were never empty. Vehicles could hardly find room to turn among the shoppers, merchants and entertainers.

Science and industry

Early China led the world in science and industry, technology and invention. Her engineering skills, developed out of the need for flood control, were unsurpassed. The Chinese began building the first irrigation reservoir in 606 BC and by the 1st century they had built the earliest arched bridge and the oldest-known iron suspension bridge. In 214 BC they completed the Great Wall, the only man-made object visible from the moon.

Considerable engineering ability was also needed for iron and salt mining. The Chinese were extracting ore, smelting it in blast furnaces, then casting it into weapons and tools about 1700 years before Europe learned the technique. Both iron and salt were so valuable, that the industries were nationalised by the Emperor Han Wu-ti in 120 BC. Silk production, although China's oldest and most lucrative industry, never became a state monopoly.

The Chinese also excelled in astronomy and other sciences. They had a calendar which was still being consulted in 1927, and sun-

Chang Heng's seismograph
The dragons point in eight directions. If an earthquake occurred, an internal pendulum caused a mechanism to vibrate so that a ball fell from one dragon's mouth into that of a toad below. An attendant recorded the direction of the tremor.

Producing salt (right)
Salt was being mined in western China by 200 BC. Deep bore-holes were drilled and brine, or salty water, was drawn up into a tank. It was carried by bamboo pipelines to pans where the water was heated and evaporated, leaving salt crystals.

The silk industry
Mulberry leaves were grown to feed the silk worm grubs. Once they had spun their silk cocoons, the insects were killed and the delicate thread was carefully unwound onto reels and then spun into silk.

Gathering mulberries

Feeding the silk worms

Drying cocoons

18

dials and water clocks. By the Han period they had measured the moon's orbit and charted over 1100 stars. Chinese observations of sun spots were almost a thousand years in advance of western records. Eclipses could be predicted and Chang Heng, a brilliant astronomer and mathematician, had invented the seismograph to record earthquakes. Han physicians were practising acupuncture, a method of healing by piercing the skin at certain points with needles. They had identified 360 vital points on the human body, only 90 less than acupuncturists use today.

Some Chinese inventions actually changed the course of history. Han paper, made from tree bark, hemp, rags and fishing nets had a tremendous impact on the growth of literacy when it finally reached Europe in the 9th century. Three Chinese inventions of the Middle Ages – printing, the magnetic compass and gunpowder – transformed civilised society. There were many other inventions, such as the wheelbarrow, the collar and harness for animals and the long cavalry stirrup which bear less dramatic witness to the superiority of Chinese technology.

Spinning silk from cocoons

Weaving the silk

Dyeing the silk

19

The exquisite arts

The first flowering of Chinese art was inspired by religion and ritual. About 5000 BC, Stone Age people placed their dead children in pottery urns, and in the following centuries increasingly elaborate objects were made for burial in tombs. Translucent jade rings, carved axe heads and daggers found in early graves display superb craftsmanship. The Ch'in, Han and later dynasties substituted graceful models in their tombs for the live sacrifices that had been made at Shang funerals. Their pottery figures of servants and bronze models of horses are cast in exquisite detail. Han tombs were also furnished with lacquered tables, boxes, trays and dishes and the walls were covered with engraved stone slabs, pressed pottery tiles or paintings. The scenes depicted in these wall paintings were often enjoyable occasions – dances, musical entertainments, meals, even official processions.

The rituals associated with ancestor worship produced beautiful objects too. The Shang reverence for their dead rulers was magnificently expressed in the bronzes characteristic of this period. Offerings of food or wine were prepared in special vessels elaborately decorated with mythical beasts and formal patterns. The early history of bronze is still an unsolved mystery, as no archaeological evidence exists of an experimental stage before the sudden appearance of these sophisticated Shang vessels.

The stone of Heaven
Jade is highly prized in Chinese tradition, not only for its beauty, but also for its magical properties. It was believed to prevent corpses decaying and a jade *pi*, a perforated disc like the one illustrated, was often buried with the dead. In the Shang period a *pi* symbolised Heaven. Rare, and also difficult to carve because of its extreme hardness, jade became a sign of wealth and power.

The ceramic art
Fine pottery vessels have been made in China since the Stone Age. At first the clay was shaped by hand, but by 2000 BC men were using the potter's wheel to turn out symmetrical vases and urns. The clay was fired in kilns of an advanced design and painted with black-and-white patterns. In Han times coloured pigments were used and a mineral called feldspar was applied to the clay before firing to produce a glazed surface. Later, T'ang craftsmen created brilliantly coloured, highly-glazed pottery vessels by adding feldspar to the clay before moulding. Under the Sung and Ming dynasties the techniques of glazing and decorative design reached a peak of perfection. Sung craftsmen created technically advanced porcelain bowls and vases with hard, lustrous glazes. Their works were in demand throughout the Far East and even the Arab world. During the Ming period (AD 1368–1644) the art of porcelain decoration reached its height in richly-coloured wares.

A painted pottery huntsman with an unruly cheetah

A glazed pottery tomb guardian

A pottery figure of a woman

Early painted jar

20

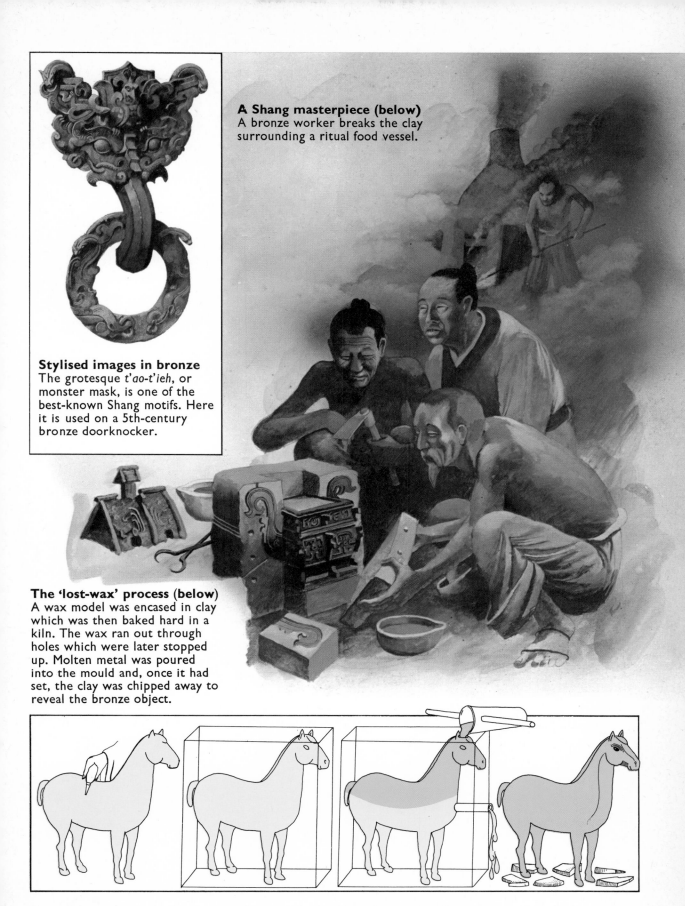

Stylised images in bronze
The grotesque *t'ao-t'ieh*, or monster mask, is one of the best-known Shang motifs. Here it is used on a 5th-century bronze doorknocker.

A Shang masterpiece (below)
A bronze worker breaks the clay surrounding a ritual food vessel.

The 'lost-wax' process (below)
A wax model was encased in clay which was then baked hard in a kiln. The wax ran out through holes which were later stopped up. Molten metal was poured into the mould and, once it had set, the clay was chipped away to reveal the bronze object.

The power of the brush

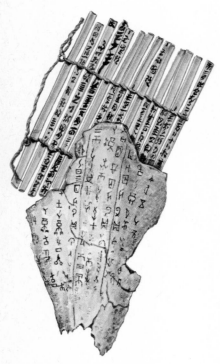

The origin of writing
Fu Hsi, a mythical emperor of China, is said to have invented Chinese writing after studying the marks on a tortoise shell, and creating 8 basic symbols.

The script in practice
Oracle bones, used in predicting the future, bear the earliest-known examples of Chinese writing. Part of a book of bamboo strips is also shown above.

No civilisation has remained so faithful to its written language as that of the Chinese. Even though pronunciation has changed radically over the centuries, modern Chinese writing is much the same as the system standardised in 213 BC by the first Ch'in emperor, Shih Huang-ti. Chinese is the oldest script in the world still in use.

Chinese writing is based on a large number of characters, or symbols, each one representing an object or idea. This is called an ideographic system and in some ways resembles Arabic numerals. Speakers of Russian or English will understand the meaning of 'five' if it is written as the figure 5, despite the fact that the word is pronounced differently. The meaning of each Chinese character has remained fixed in the same way. Thus, unlike the speaker of any other modern language, a Chinese is able to read the literature his ancestors wrote a thousand years ago.

The most primitive elements of the Chinese script were pictographs, or simple drawings, similar to Egyptian hieroglyphs. Each was a stylised picture of a familiar object, such as a horse or a mountain. Gradually the scope of the written language was widened by making individual parts stand for a whole: a group of trees, for instance, represented a forest. The script was further extended by combining two or more pictographs. Thus the sign for 'wife' was made up of the symbols for 'woman', 'hand' and 'broom'. Although modern characters evolved over a long period of time, about 2000 of these early pictographs are still in use in a recognisable form. The sign for 'tiger', for example, has kept the distinct tail of the original symbol:

China's first written records are inscriptions on Shang oracle bones and shells. Before making important decisions, the Shang kings asked the advice of supernatural powers through a priest who drilled a hole in a piece of tortoiseshell or bone, then heated it until the surface cracked. Using a sharp stylus, or cutting tool, he wrote down the questions, then the answers, which he interpreted from the pattern of cracks.

Brushes of deer's hair were being used for writing by Han times. Government orders and tax records were made on wood or bamboo but valuable scientific works or poetry and prose for the palace library were painted on silk. The Han period also saw the invention of paper which eventually came into general use for book production. There was tremendous literary activity at this time. New literary forms and styles were created. There were short, lyrical poems and longer descriptive accounts of life at court. Hymns, wedding chants and folk poetry of the Imperial Age provided models for later writers. Ssu-ma Ch'ien wrote the first comprehensive history of China in about 100 BC, a work describing the history of man in the world which formed a model for later historians, and in AD 121 the first dictionary appeared. T'ang scribes wrote down standard versions of these ancient writings on fine paper which they rolled on to sandalwood or ivory cylinders tipped with rock crystal, jade or ivory.

The power of the brush
Calligraphy, or the art of beautiful hand-writing, did not develop until the sharp writing tools of the Shang dynasty had been abandoned for the brush. By Han times brush painting had transformed writing from a formal skill into a refined and complex means of self-expression. Calligraphers were regarded as artists and many of their tools reflect the nobility of their craft. The illustration shows two graceful brushes, one made of jade, the other of painted porcelain and a carbon-black ink cake which is impressed with a delicate design.

Calligraphers studied their art for many years. They learned to hold the brush firmly at a vertical and never to rest their elbows on the table. There were eight basic strokes to perfect, all of which were combined in the character for *yung*, meaning eternity. There is a legend that Wang Hsi-chih, a brilliant calligrapher of the 4th century, practised for 15 years to master this one character.

The concept and technique of brush writing, is very like that of painting. The Chinese painter and calligrapher used the same inks and fine brushes to express themselves on silk or paper. Brush parties, like the one below, were enjoyable occasions. Learned men drank wine and competed with one another to complete stanzas of poetry. They were liberally supplied with piles of white paper, brushes and black ink (being mixed by a boy here).

Artistry on silk
Silk production is China's oldest luxury industry. Chinese silk was sold on the Roman markets in the later Han period. Embroidering silk onto plain fabric was a highly developed art. Above is a painting on silk, probably executed in north-west China.

23

Three ways

Taoism was founded by Lao-tzu, 'The Old Philosopher', seen here riding a water buffalo.

Buddhism
In the late Han period, Indian missionaries brought the word of Buddha, the 'Enlightened One', to China. They taught a religion based on meditation and calm detachment from worldly hopes and possessions. Their belief in reincarnation, or man's constant birth and rebirth into human or animal form, was new to China. By the 6th century the religion had been accepted along with the native teachings of Taoism and Confucianism.

China is unique among the great empires of the ancient world in absorbing several quite distinct religions and allowing them to exist in harmony together. The Early Chinese worshipped ancestors as well as gods of Nature. Later, the practical teachings of Confucius thrived alongside the mystical religions of Taoism and Buddhism. To the Chinese there was nothing inconsistent in following all three beliefs: Confucianism, Taoism and Buddhism were regarded simply as 'three ways to one goal'.

Ancestor worship was the oldest and most enduring religion in China. The Shang kings consulted their royal forefathers on important matters and from the Han period onwards, all Chinese families worshipped their ancestors. Early Chinese also revered the spirits of Nature. Through a special priest or priestess called a shaman, who spoke to the spirits in a trance, the peasants prayed to the god of the Yellow River, to the Earth god, or to the spirits of mountains, trees and lakes.

These primitive religions continued to flourish but they did not satisfy people in times of great trouble. During the Warring States period which led up to the First Empire, scholars travelled from state to state, presenting their ideas of the right way to live to any lord or king who would listen. Two of the greatest Chinese thinkers, Confucius and Lao-tzu taught during this period. So many theories about the true meaning of life were put forward at this time that they were known as the 'Hundred Schools'. Apart from Legalism, which flourished briefly under the Ch'in Dynasty, the teachings of Confucius and Lao-tzu were the only two of the 'Hundred Schools' to survive these unsettled times.

24

Confucius (551–479 BC) was born into an aristocratic family in the state of Lu, in the modern province of Shantung. He spent most of his life teaching a practical way of life that should be called a philosophy, or way of thinking, rather than a religion. Confucius emphasised loyalty, sincerity, courtesy and respect for parents as the proper code of conduct for everyone. He believed that official posts should be held, not because of a man's birth or wealth, but by virtue of talent and education. Under the Han Dynasty, this belief led to a system of state examinations for civil servants. The teachings of Confucius continued to influence Chinese education, government and social life for two thousand years.

Taoists, in direct contrast to the Confucian school, followed a more passive way of life, intent on cultivating inner powers and living in harmony with Nature. They believed in 'tao', or the natural 'way' to truth, rather than in an ordered government of laws and rigid authority. Many Taoists withdrew from society to contemplate the wisdom and peace of Nature, hoping that they would eventually become immortal and live in paradise. However, the early experiments of the Taoist alchemists laid the foundations of Chinese science.

Buddhism was not well established in China before the T'ang Dynasty, but by then emperors had begun to support the new religion and sculptors were making magnificent images of its gods. Taoism and Buddhism were both mystical religions and, although all three major doctrines co-existed quite comfortably, Chinese government and education remained Confucian.

Legalism
The Legalist school of thought believed that noble behaviour and good deeds would never improve either government or society. They advised strict laws and brutal punishments instead. Ch'in Shih Huang-ti, the First Emperor, supported the Legalist doctrine. He banned all other philosophies and ordered their written teachings to be burned. Happily, Legalism did not outlast Ch'in rule. In Han times scholars re-wrote the books of early philosophers.

Confucius, shown here, taught a philosophy based on good conduct.

25

Family life

The most important institution in China was the family. Under the Han Dynasty it was the basic unit of all levels of society, from the humble peasants up to the emperor himself. Every child was taught to honour his parents. Obedience to his father was directly related to the ancient religion of ancestor worship. Some of the Han emperors set up shrines to their ancestors in the provinces as well as the capital city and appointed priests and guards to look after them. It was believed that when a man died, his spirit could influence the fate of his descendants on earth. The family could expect to obtain the goodwill of their dead ancestors only by offering them food and wine and by praying to their spirits at special altars kept in Chinese homes for that purpose.

It was thought that the goodwill thus obtained could bring the family many blessings: luxurious houses and carriages for the aristocratic classes; for the peasants, simply enough food and clothing. Rich families furnished their houses with lacquered tables, bronze mirrors, paintings and imported cashmere carpets. They feasted on exotic dishes like snails preserved in vinegar, dogmeat and tangerines. Food was served on fine porcelain and eaten with elegant wooden chopsticks. Wine, coconut milk and fermented palm juice were drunk out of goblets made of beaten silver or gold. Wealthy men and women wore silk tunics and jackets, brocade slippers and gold ornaments in their hair.

The peasant existed on millet cakes, rice, beans, turnips and fish. He wore clothes woven from hemp and straw sandals.

Ancestor worship
The Shang paid homage only to dead kings but by Han times every family made offerings at altars dedicated to their ancestors.

Music and musicians
One of these wooden figures, from a tomb a little after the Han period, is a pan-pipes player and the other has a three-stringed zither. They would have played in small orchestral groups of four or five. Rich people owned their own musicians.

The leisure hours
Chinese children played jack stones and shuttlecock. Adults of wealthy families enjoyed board games similar to modern lotto and backgammon. Here is a game of the Han period called *liu po*, played by throwing sticks and moving pieces around the board.

Seasonal celebrations
Festivals were for rich and poor alike. Amusements included sport, music, dancing and spectacles of kite-flying, a Chinese invention of the 3rd century BC.

Cheating death

The jade Prince
The body of Han Liu Sheng was buried in a suit made from 2498 pieces of jade, a magical stone to the Chinese. It probably took ten years to make.

Early Chinese houses were built of wood and mud-brick. Not one of them has survived to tell us about styles of architecture, furniture or household utensils. But information about the living has been provided by the dead whose tombs, hewn from solid rock or built of stone, have endured for centuries.

Shang Dynasty tombs have revealed magnificent bronze vessels and carved limestone figures, although the burial chambers themselves have often been plundered. Shang ritual funerals were reserved for kings alone, and offerings were on a lavish scale. Jade ornaments, bronze weapons and cauldrons, carved bone and ivory, painted pottery and musical instruments were buried with human and animal sacrifices. Sometimes hundreds of men bowed their heads to the executioner's axe and on at least one occasion an entire zoo of animals was slaughtered.

Most of these grave gifts were buried in the main pit-tomb. This was a deep shaft resembling an inverted pyramid sunk 30 or 40 feet into the ground. The main approach to the tomb was from the south along a sloping ramp, and steep stairs led into the pit from the other three directions. Sometimes the ramps were guarded by dead sentries armed with bronze weapons. Once the ceremonial

rites had been completed, the shaft was filled in with earth.

Soon after the collapse of the Shang Dynasty, the practice of human sacrifice was forgotten. The Chou, their conquerors, buried models in graves and from the Han period onwards, small clay figures were substituted for men and animals. But now important officials and wealthy families began to build elaborate tombs cut into cliffs or made of stone. Family reverence for ancestors led naturally to a general concern for ancestral graves. There were no public cemeteries in China – even the poorest people buried their dead on free land by the river or outside city walls.

Royal tombs were the most extravagant. The twin, rock-cut tombs of Prince Liu Sheng and his wife, Princess Tou Wan, who died in the 2nd century BC, could each hold 1000 people. Both were filled with objects of bronze, gold, silver, jade, stone and pottery and lacquer-work. Their most spectacular treasures were the jade suits worn by the royal pair. Each was made from over 2000 rectangles of polished jade sewn together with gold wire. But the magic jade, symbol of heaven, supposed to protect bodies from decay, failed to preserve the Prince and Princess: only their dust remains.

29

'Let the past serve the present'

The Great Wall

Although China is a vast country, it is well protected from the outside world by a combination of mountains to the west, jungles to the south, and the sea to the east. Only the open steppelands of the north have been exposed to the repeated raids of barbarian horsemen. In order to repel these uninvited guests, Shih Huan-ti, first emperor of the Ch'in dynasty, marshalled thousands of *nung* to labour for years, connecting three earlier walls into the formidable defence system we know as the Great Wall. It ran for 2400 miles. The Wall failed only to keep out the Mongols, and the Manchus.

Chinese civilisation has flourished continuously for over 3500 years. Although the ancient imperial system came to an end in 1912, when the last of the Manchu emperors was deposed, the People's Republic of China has maintained many of the great traditions of the past. The Communist Revolution itself fits into the historic Chinese pattern of rebellion against harsh or ineffectual rulers. Mao Tse-tung, as leader of the Republic, set in motion an active investigation of history through archaeology with the words, 'Let the past serve the present'.

In June 1968, soldiers working on a limestone hill near Man-ch'eng, uncovered the tombs of the Han Prince, Liu Sheng, who died in 113 BC, and his wife, Princess Tou Wan. Both tombs were filled with hoards of precious objects.

This discovery was so unique that news of it reached the rest of the world in less than two years. Soon afterwards, China allowed the greater part of the priceless treasure to be exhibited in the west for the first time.

Of course, many other sites have been excavated besides these two. Most excavations have been carried out since the People's Republic was established in 1949, and during the Cultural Revolution nearly 500,000 historical objects were added to the collections in Chinese museums. Perhaps Chinese archaeology will continue to bring east and west closer despite the invisible barrier which, in modern times, has replaced the ancient one of the Great Wall.

Index